Could Be

Cover art: Craig Carlisle *Full Moon Rising* (oil on linen)
Author photo: Marc Ross

ISBN: 978-1-962405-65-2

Sheila-Na-Gig Editions
Russell, KY
Hayley Mitchell Haugen, Editor
www.sheilanagigblog.com

Printed in the United States of America

Could Be

Poems

Rikki Santer

Sheila-Na-Gig Editions

Advance Praise

Rikki Santer's new collection *Could Be,* is a masterful balance of both experiences seemingly bereft of hope, and those revealing portals of light that nudge the reader firmly into otherwise. Yet near the book's beginning, in the poem "Childhood Gothic," Santer also offers a foundation, a lesson rooted in resilience: "Down the street where I grew up, lived an elderly neighbor who adored bones. Her guest / room was a playground for memories of flesh," and at the poem's conclusion, "…It was then I was schooled in the delights of uncanny and for what's left / over when the future comes after you. She'd tell me to listen for angels that come down / from their ladders. I'd nod and whisper into every eye hole." Therein lie tangible bones of loss, with light filtering in from each eye hole.

Throughout *Could Be,* despair waltzes in tandem with redemption: "Sometimes we are whimpering wounds" but "ancient mercies linger." There are moments when a page aches but never is there a line of resignation—"when I say I don't know anything anymore I mean the compass / is confused by its own magnetism, road ahead or road behind? / and when I say magnetism I mean the safety lock forgot / its password and all words have passed their expiration dates / but I do hold a key, many thanks…"

Could Be is a triumph. Like Santer's other collections, this book challenges and dazzles the reader's mind with stunning images and unique turns of language. Epiphanies are abundant throughout. Rikki Santer is a virtuoso with every poem she undertakes.

—Sandra Feen; 2022-2024 Ohio Beat Poet Laureate,
author of *Evidence of Starving*

Those familiar with Rikki Santer's poetry will know her to be a word wizard, one who conjures fresh, clever imagery and sound to cast a spell on the reader. In her latest collection, *Could Be,* Santer again applies these talents to address the powerlessness we feel in our struggles to face darkness and its evolution, both personal and communal. From the "dark loop of dementia" to the "corrosive syllables of bulldozer and chainsaw" to "family dinners with thorns in the pudding," no experience is off limits. Santer deftly journeys between past, present, and future, exploring familiar themes of loss—and our memory of it—and hope, and how they imprint themselves on "the parchment of humankind." She offers suggestions, if not solutions, for finding comfort in the natural world, the salve of nostalgia, and "the oldest songs on our planet." More importantly, Santer reminds us of the unexpected angels we can rely on to help us sift through the "bitter archives of human failings" that litter our relationships and to discover the potential of our better selves.

—Chuck Salmons, author of *Surviving the Eremocene*

Acknowledgments

Ark Review: "198 McNaughton"

BarBar & 3rd place Ohio Poetry Association Eco Poem Competition: "This and That"

Birds of the Cuyahoga, 2022 Edith Chase Anthology: "Thought. Song."

Blood & Bourbon: "Fry"

Blue Rivers: "Unassuming in New Jersey"

The Brussels Review: "Bon Appetit," "Grinnell Mill B&B That Week," "The Spell of Letters"

Common Threads (Ohio Poetry Association): "Session"

Concision Poetry Journal: "Swallower"

A Confluence of Poems: A Tribute to Tributaries, 2025 Edith Chase Poetry Anthology & Finalist for the Maxine Cassin Poetry Prize from the Poetry Society of Louisiana: "Bluebells"

CrayfishMag: "Now"

Dark Winter Literary Review: "Proceed to the Route," "Some Playing With Dozens"

Hellbender Magazine: "What Scares the Candy Corn Out of Me"

Hood of Bone Review: "Suburban Creatures With a Line From Jean Valentine"

I-70 Review: "Mad-Cat de Pompadour," "Sip"

The Ilanot Review: "Could Be"

JAKE: "Department Store"

January House Literary Journal: "No, But," "Session"

Main Street Rag: "Like There's No Tomorrow"

Main Street Rag, North Coast Voices Anthology: "Currency of Taste"

TheNewVerse.News & *The Going-Away Country* (Kattywompus Press): "Invasive Species"

Nine Mile Magazine: "Libretto Gymnastics," "Poeming Through"

North Dakota Quarterly: "Interrogation"

Northhampton Poetry Review: "Everything"

Pan Haiku Review: "Any Door"

Pangyrus: "I'm Probably Not"

Ponder Review: "How Should a Woman Sound"

Quotidian Bagatelle: "Living Like a Trickster Inside the Truck"
Red Wolf Journal: "Two of Us"
Santa Fe Literary Review: "My Peripatetic Father"
Sheila-Na-Gig online: "Thought. Song."
Silver Birch Press: "Breath of Things," "Visitor's Log"
SLAB: "Donald Duck on the Couch"
The Soliloquist: "Almost Pantoum for the Myth of Certainty," "Fall Equinox at Geneva-on-the-Lake," "Night Geometries"
Streetcake: "Planethood"
The Westchester Review: "Food Storage"
Whale Road Review & nominated for Best Small Fictions sponsored by Alternating Current Press: "Childhood Gothic"
The Willow Review: "Creekside," "High School Reunion During Jell-O Mold and Cheese Platter"
Yearling: "Dream Glosa"

In Gratitude

Thank you to all the generous editors of journals who believed in these poems and delivered them into the world, and for the ants and angels who made many appearances in this crop of poems.

I am grateful for the local poetry community that sustains me, especially the following writers who for this collection, gifted me with insightful feedback, always knowing just when to push and just when to pull: Sayuri Ayers, Kathleen Burgess, Sandra Feen, Louise Robertson, Mikelle Hickman-Romine, Chuck Salmons, and all the thoughtful folks from the Salon and Bistro writing groups.

I am indebted to Sandra Feen, Kari Gunter-Seymour, Chuck Salmons, and Sara Moore Wagner for the generosity of their time and attention and for the artistry of their words to frame the energy of this collection.

Much gratitude to artist Craig Carlisle who so easily agreed to lend an image of his painting, "Full Moon Rising" that graces the cover. I adore its bold sense of meditative longing as it introduces this collection.

I am forever grateful for Marc who has steadied me for a lifetime. You are my first reader and my patient, sounding board, whose unflinching support and encouragement has championed my dreams.

Thank you, thank you, Hayley Mitchell Haugen, founder and editor of Sheila-Na-Gig Editions, for that first conversation at AWP when you invited me to submit a new manuscript for your consideration. Your astute editing has rendered this collection with artfulnesss and integrity; I am honored to now be a member of the Sheila-Na-Gig family.

And for my sweet son, I dedicate this collection to you, the purest love I've known.

None of my worldings measure
up no crazy between the ears no
identity pain nailed to my
skull no vicious
ideas no housed rage no
wronged heritage pacing
in the wings no sticky
schoolbooks flimflammery
or swallowtailed anything
no bruised tongue no broken
drunks no tracked
arms no shivering
in back alleys no sweaty
I'll kill you
if you tell
no bullets no
knives no
fire flood blood
fragments of war.
No my fables step back
teetering on the edges
of themselves
my small country
at the top of the hour.

Contents

Session

The psychologist's dogs wear diapers
as they parade around the office like Slinkys,
one Shih Tzu to offset incontinence
one Pomeranian to sanction equity.

Outside off-key notes bristle treeshadows,
wingshadows, rattletrap recipe from twilight,
upside down sky in my teacup, a few geese
bark across its span, crows perch around its rim.

I sip and starlings flap between my teeth,
please marry me to hope, that gap between
currency of hammock and what flickers
in the mind. In this suite a wind chime's

distant bells. Pause unwraps another bonbon
of relief with a pictorial turn above the couch
in the shimmering/trembling globe of Chardin's
soap bubble, mirror for the filigree of me wanting

to be heard to not, yearning for release
from the pluck and tuck of retelling.
Out back, around the lake, it's eclipse
plumage season for mallards, their bright

green heads molting, biding time
to take flight again. Shih Tzu nests
in my lap, growly sort of purr, tail
wagging like a determined metronome.

I walk to my car, childhood kite bobbing
through the weight of the wind, next
appointment card in my back pocket,
the steady first star of Venus.

Childhood Gothic

Down the street where I grew up lived an elderly neighbor who adored bones. Her guest room was a playground for memories of flesh. With death tangy in my mouth, I'd sneak over for lemon bars and the chance to rub my fingers over immortality, caressing its things that could be seen and smelled. Shelves and tabletops were crowded with calcified clocks for time—pelvises in dark patina, platters of teeth or vertebrae, crusted skulls in drop jaw still life, and swaying in her closet, an oddfellow skeleton I named Stinky Cheeseman after my favorite book. It was then I was schooled in the delights of uncanny and for what's left over when the future comes after you. She'd tell me to listen for angels that come down from their ladders. I'd nod and whisper into every eye hole.

Invasive Species

Sometimes a jackass
is just a jackass
a president once said
when he thought
no one was listening.
And some say
that when God
created the world
he dispatched an angel
with a sack of fools
to distribute
one per town,
but the harvest of folly
seems plentiful these days
with its dangerous parable staining.

Tiny phones
in their back pockets
to showcase glowing selfies
and toothy tweets,
all these Looney Tunes legislators
who always have a guy
or know where to get one.
And they fantasize
about winning more
epic battles between
the us and them
or want-to versus should-have.
Beneath the peels,
so many sad bananas
vying for the pratfalls
of others.
Beneath their blindfolds,

they swing hard
at political piñatas
with tantrums
of taketh away.

Too late to send them
to their rooms to think
of what they've done
or have them vulcanized
when Mars attacks.
Their heads brim
with knuckles clenched,
feverous for playing
again and again
their most favorite game—
capture the flag.
And now fat-fingered justices
join in.

Could Be

Like a julienned potato
light cuts through window slats
and I realize I'm in the opening scene
of *Click Bait for Dots Connecting*
because it's noon and my bed wants to know
if I'm getting up already
but it's the skin of memory
when an overheated mind begins cantering
with the hem and haw of nearby you and you
and you which ruptures the room
galloping a gajillion miles a minute.
Last night, cheek on my husband's chest
his iambic melody thumping
with a new butterfly plug that fills
the small hole that could have been the gateway
for the stroke that caused us to pray for a deadline extension.
Phone call from friend my age
in despair's dark loop of dementia.
Downstairs son's inner child frayed and broken
teetering on canyon's rim.
And I am lost in grids of empty faces
the corkscrew of cable news
frisson of a new administration's dangerous batshit
genocide of distant babies and children.
The pulse the vapor
of this chockablock putting two
and ten and twenty together leaves me with what's inescapable.
I am here. Right here
with the sourdough starter
bubbling its sour salvo in the kitchen.

Fall Equinox at Geneva-on-the-Lake

There's a necklace of gulls near the shore,
each with a thing or two to say as they

preach atop their own head of rock.
I think of the ancient medicine wheels

where the Sioux marked time in vast skies
of the great plains. Here, at the soothing lips

of Lake Erie, the balance of light and dark
summons my thoughts of you. So many times

when I had lingered marveling at a tiny you sleeping
with crossed ankles, nested in the expanse of mattress,

I'd pray you'd be cradled in a lifetime of lush fields.
Now we are lost in the quotients and remainders

of our long division and I am a stranded bystander,
no longer able to help you steady the fulcrums of

your equinoxes. You have roped off your darkness,
your lightness drowns in sorrow of your making.

I greet the gulls with morsels from my hoagie.
They swirl and dip as the Sun and Earth align.

I text you an image of a feather left behind in the sand.
LOL, you write. *Looks like a quill for more of your more.*

Interrogation

Never mind my muscle tension, galvanic skin responses, or my tongue slipping because I remember that day was bland like a bowl of under-spiced pudding, and there's absolutely no doubt that I meant well as the restraining order must have been eaten by my chihuahua and I really don't mind your obsession with my fingerprints on her *mirror mirror on the wall* and sure I'm not the brightest knife in the drawer but I admit I have always been a fan of the clandestine, but only in comic books and movies, yet I want to state clearly and without qualification that mistakes must have been made but it could not have been me because I've lost my lucky rat's tail and I never go out without it and then there's the audacity of a crow that stole my car keys that afternoon and it really offends me that you would accuse me of something like that because if I could flower I would flourish with a PhD in loving color and I promise you that I was not on the run, on the sly, or in any time frame not accounted for, plus I'm someone you'd probably like to know so my fortune teller has advised me against saying any more and thanks for asking, but I'm just swine—I mean I'm just udderly, unequivocally fine.

Grinnell Mill B&B That Week

From the opened window of the guesthouse
a congress of strung keys sways
in the night breeze
like a beaded curtain,
and moonlight on my cheek
is just the right amount of fidelity.

Next to our guest bed decked
with crisp white linens
a cold bird body, its black chevron
on the oak floor with ellipses
of black ants bubbling around it.
What could the free-standing mirror
have promised this barn swallow?
Sometimes we are whimpering wounds.

At the convenience store the goose
nests her eggs atop
a parking lot island
and each day her head swivels
for cars and shoppers as they pass.

Ancient mercies linger.
One moment can only breed
another. Our last day the goose
leads her fluffy goslings
across the morning pavement.
Our last night the strung keys sing
in the evening breeze
like a curtain divine.

My Peripatetic Father

I cling to riddled clouds and try to keep up, his unlit El Producto a baton measuring the brisk beat of his gait. On my weekend visit he's asked me to join him in his three-mile routine through the neighborhood. It's the easy alphabet of his jokes and his naming of front yard flowers, the Kravitz's snapdragons his favorite. On the stove, back in their apartment kitchen, his tangy compote steeps and the shopping list on the fridge in his award-winning penmanship curls its tail. The sidewalks are his daily colonnade as he walks off his angst as caregiver for a wife whose legs no longer wanderlust. Today it's the rainy mist that saturates our joy of being together, his weathered wallet from the war in my back pocket. We stop so he can tell the mail carrier that last night he watched the original *The Postman Always Rings Twice* on Turner Classics and we all laugh because there's not a single mail carrier in the story. On the next block an owl duets with its partner across the ravine. My father takes my hand, winks, then we both jump into a puddle in the elementary school parking lot. O, that daddy of mine who likes frisking when I'm around. We round the last leg of our journey as he offers boss and boyfriend advice. With his arm around my shoulder, we're so far away from the Monday morning phone call about him.

Hospital waiting room
Code Blue over intercom
slow summer rain

198 McNaughten Road

Council approves plans for new apartment complex over concerns of Far East Side residents —Columbus Dispatch; June 27, 2024

My bike parked, I amble over your body still
sprawling as your destiny surrenders to lonely gusts
of breeze *(and the earth opened her mouth to swallow
the blood of Abel).* Your tongue severed, roots will
tremble beneath your stoic congress of trees as corrosive
syllables of bulldozer and chainsaw fill you until
your ribs crack. Blazing crotches of engine will raze
your green to black, scour every cleft and crevice,
silence your morning dew, the industry of your nests,
hives, thickets, the ranch house ghosts of trellises,
fragrant gardens, playful hymns of wind chimes.
Your three parcels will finally give way to commerce.
How much we've cost you. How much we've cost
ourselves left with impotent vowels of aftermath.

View From Here

Glory garden shriveled

to single blackened raspberry tendril.

All day bathrobe

Pillsbury Doughboy pajama pants

curls longer each week

to part his woe.

She paces

in hush of nights

for a camp

of angels

to save him.

Macaw

Neighbor favored the paradox of captivity.
She liked when her macaw
scuttled across waxed mahogany
to share morsels of berries, peaches,
raisins she gripped with arthritic fingers
to place in a circle around him.

Who's my baby?
*Who's **my** baby?*
Whose mimicry was mimicry?

The rainforest rims in his starboard eyes,
his clicks in nuzzle and coo
between piles of pinyon shells,
their weekly pilgrimages
with an umbrella stroller
to talk and squawk
in the neighborhood park,
their subsong duet for attentive children.

Widow with her blue and gold—
their lifelines dampened the will to flock,
to ply the air—still
they beguiled each other
with slow swiveling sideswipes
of gaze, the way they'd dip their heads
below their bodies and
crane upward like movie cameras.
In cerulean and goldenrod
in gingham and lace
they met each other
for sustenance and magic
in vectors of birdcall and heartbeat.

Any Door

The painter conjures. Follow him through his portal to a calligraphy of oak trees. In this crib of tranquility, you will find yourself sweetly rocking in a handwoven hammock, dioramas taking form in your head. As you doze, a book of poems slips from your fingers onto a mossy ring of toadstools while a shaft of June sunlight warms your toes. Around you a fleece-like hush takes over. A bright vanishing flashes from shade to shade and ambient menthol throngs the air. Then a soft twittering and the child you once miscarried steps from behind a weary trunk. Small fingers stroke your neck with a tender whisper. *You can fit through any door you wish.* Painting takes another breath.

Thought. Song.

Particle. Wave. The glorious inhale/
exhale of it. Two cardinals dither
daily at our address. My husband
believes that drones should be our
next state bird but I believe in you—
our backyard familiars, priestly robes
of Ohio, red beyond any of our reds.

Beneath the ceiling of your soaring,
you've stayed put in our ravine, life
mates under a Biblical edge of sky.
Together, you are the opening lines
of our mornings, schooling us
in harmony, our vowels between
your vowels.

You are the sum of our location
decorating our spring dogwood,
clear-windowed news filled
with quivering guillemots
for whom you both share
feeding with unspoken equity.

You light on our deck's railing,
leap onto our breakfast table,
porcelain plate filled with blueberries
and black-oil seeds and sometimes,
in my aptitude for stillness, mother
pecks from my palm. I think you
come close because you can escape
so easily.

This winter, swish of scarlet frosting,
black masks that seem to wait for our
notice. Children hum in the next room.
Husband brings me hot toddy.
Kiss between us, our tongues,
mealworms twirling for sustenance.
Where we've been doesn't matter.
Where we fit so perfectly grows wings.

Department Store

To swallow the world before it swallows us, why shopping
gladdens the heart. This palace, giant cubist cupcake, frontier

that feels like a poem about everything. Escalators deliver
our giraffing necks in honeyed waves. We're so many faces

with lustful topographies, credit cards in our holsters all in the high beams of stuff
displayed exponentially. Decapitated mannequins hum anthems as their fingers point

the way. So many labyrinths racks of chainmail & glistening
counters of magic potions declare the deepest deep of discount.

It's a pagan chant of neckties splayed across lucite tables,
the many altars of brave stilettos, felted pom-pom trivets

& astronaut lunchbags claiming that their whole selves freeze.
Pan's midnight flute our Muzak, chattering buck moons at every

make-up mirror has us blooming before our leaves are destined to fall.
Clearance racks packed tight & spilling last chances,

deep-pile couches & big cabbage roses lure us into bathroom lounges
of movie-set lavish to flaunt our bounty. And then

when we finally depart this multi-tiered Mecca through doors that spin into concrete towers
we pause to ponder which plane of existence we parked on.

Some Playing With Dozens

my tongue encircles each stale crueller in its carton like a
thought experiment deep in the folds of memory

every soiled month of that year you swung back and forth from
a trapeze of your own making

a dozen noons and midnights of spitting blame

your headpiece of antlers made twelve points that could not be
denied in the courtroom

the baker's dozen of my misgivings lodged in the boughs of
spring's cottonwood tree

your face cards that dragnetted and salted the navel of what lost
its tenderness

a platter of deviled yokes surrendered that morning after the wake

your delusions are so illusory, your charades have squirming
tendrils

your neediness is so arrogant, its cruise ship has no lifeboats

your bouquet of roses was so mistaken, it could be a banished
angel stripped of its wings

apostles dispersed in waves to leave this earth to endless
questions

release of six couples to the clouds, church of doves

Bon Appétit* As Political Pundit: A Cento (Issue May 2024):

> **Bon Appétit,* a monthly American food and entertaining magazine has been appearing since 1956, the year of Operation Redwing, the first air-deployed thermonuclear weapons test by the United States, and when the movie *The 10 Commandments* premiered.

What I'm loving
has a long history
way beyond creamy pasta.
Honey, I brought the goods
by poaching
more is more.
Excess is the point.
Don't mess around when it comes to
humongous internet imposters
cut in precise soldier-like planks
and seasoned with a complex web
of cheeky and dirty.
Skin side up,
it all pairs nicely
with a twist that turns.
And yes, it can overcook quickly
so keep an eye on the hyper-regional
that's low on effort
taking cues from shortcuts
like a slurry
of boxed and bagged
cores of spiky.
So tag it. Swizzle it.
There's more than enough
bracing clarity
as it all simmers
in its firm and meaty texture
towards the last
Last Call.

Libretto Gymnastics

Fellows Riverside Gardens; Youngstown, Ohio

Usually it's a lot of people in costumes, falling
in love or seduction, dying in someone's arms,

and of course, all that singing. Here in the middle
of the day it's a cascade of bubbles egging on

a squirming toddler, camera-not-ready atop
a staged block of hay. And it's the aria

of a mylar balloon waltzing in the embrace
of a tall pine and saluting the struggling

steel mill valley below. This hometown visit disrobes
my awkward past to pull me into my present and

suddenly I feel all silky, finger-snapping my way
down a meandering path of scarecrows each coming

to life with cartoon heads and straw-stuffed limbs
decked in filigree and angel wings. From the iridescent

dialects of crows, a surge of jubilee as the blood
and bone pirouettes of two chipmunks stir a crispy

carpet of leaves. If this poem could *Bahm Bahm Bahm Bahmmmmm*
it would, and here I am restrung by the rhapsody of early

fall breeze and the perfumed vortex of grove after grove
of rosebush virtuosos in colorful rapture of bud and bloom.

Food Storage

Your disdain releases a pint of tapeworms.
You, weary of finding yet
another expired package on our shelves,
cheese mold on its way to science fiction,
a spatula whispering rust.

We joke, you scowl.
You lean into our sauce jars with bloodhound intensity.
Sugary excuses never fill you.
Our cartoons on the fridge never close to witty.

We, your Greek tragedy, guilty of habitual gluten and dairy.
You, our oldest and youngest,
whose tender slumber we carried from the car seat,
whose merry cackles jumped into our arms from behind bushes,
who relished his soupy goopy Lucky Charms and mashed
potato towers.

Now it's the sour simmer of your visits,
your squall and snipe for our long-gone, best-if-used-bys.
You, the relentless garbage disposal autocrat at our sink.
We, the family dinners with thorns in the pudding.

Then a decade-old can of tomato paste
at the back of our pantry
bursts open its blood along the seam,
and absolution leaves the building.

Mad-Cat de Pompadour

with gratitude to Nia Gould
and her book, *A History of Art in 21 Cats*

There was no sign of diva-tude
when she showed up at our door
straggly and famished. Two days
of tuna and slumber and there
she was pirouetting around the house
testing boundaries atop boundaries,
bookcases, the washing machine.
If she fits, she sits.
Pointillist in pools of sunlight,
she knows how to disappear
and when feeling shady, claws
us in our sleep. Zoomies during
Zoom meetings, our wild beast
with Van Dogen eyes, chattering
and gnawing in Dadaist splendor.
Her nose tangoes with the aquarium's
flying fish. The couch's afghan
her floral headpiece. Clouds in her eyes,
she crouches, Artemis in a potted
plant jungle. Our Jacklyn Pollock
of muddy paw prints and doodly
Keith Haring whiskers glittering
catnip. Yes, she has bewitched
us with her intoxicating charms,
so we charged it to be delivered
next week in black cherry,
a La Belle Epoque cat bed with
sculpted wisteria embellishments
and a bespoke cushion covered with
luxurious lemongrass chenille.

Suburban Creatures With a Line From Jean Valentine

The curl of a baby deer's   gutted body   now beneath

a circle of stones   in a backyard grave   *life from whom death*

springeth green.   Taut wire   between fawn   and coyote

in the night   howl and hot teeth   that pursued   a wobbly run

stumble   then church   of bent grass   damp   with blood

and the vigorous beaks of vultures   to swallow

two new eyes   this morning's   front lawn.

I'm Probably Not

what you're looking for,
my panties drawer crammed
with random
monogrammed hankies
that I shoplift from
thrift stores and on days
off I like to draw mustaches
with permanent marker
on all the honey
bear bottles at coffee
shops around town
and yep I keep a diary of quotes
from my favorite sardonic
TV judges and with my
morning prune juice smoothie
I relish watching footage loops
of fireworks, you know the kind
that looks like it's raining spermatozoa
and I'm serious when I tell you
that I would have your favorite
knock-knock joke tattooed
around my left wrist to answer
the right one, so as I am two
people behind you waiting
for the carousel, transmitting
thought waves into your cranium
so that you will choose swan
boat and I will mount
palomino and when
the sparkling music begins
we will twirl and twirl as
if we are riding in our very own

snow globe and we will suck
our clouds of cotton candy
until our brains melt and
leak right out of our ears.

Visitor's Log

Shoring up fragments, our convention
of black ants punctuates their messages

across the space-time of our bathroom
tile floor, many vrooming by too fast

to be snagged by elegy but miracles
arise from the mundane. We, too,

are foragers bound for something
somewhere so we cup-a-bug the ones

that we can and carry them to the front
door. In the kitchen, another tribe claims

the counter—their red mass busy
in sliced honeydewed ecstacy. These,

the wildlife we know best. What
the conniving spider weaves at the

yawning juncture of our bedroom
baseboards and the whirr of a fly

within the beam of my book light.
Alas, my sieve of dream-state

against the prattle of cable news
refuses to conjure so I move to

the living room to find myself
reflected in the sliding glass door

looking in from the ravine where I like
learning the business of bats in moonlight

and listening for the walls of melody
to swell from the katydids—those

leaves that come to life—scraping
out the oldest songs on our planet.

What Scares the Candy Corn Out of Me

Bigfoot runs for office, wins my state's Congressional seat
and fulfills his pledge for an eagle drumstick in every pot.

SPIRIT Pop-up Halloween superstores never move out
and transmogrify into school uniform outlets.

Small town lamppost banners suspended across the nation
feature MAGA insurrectionists as hometown heroes.

My city's water department flavors the fluoride
with pumpkin spice.

All NFL, NBA, and MLB owners replace pre-game singing
of the national anthem with The Monster Mash.

Chocolate tarantulas abound with gauntlets of painful
puckering from Cry Baby Tears Extra Sour gumballs.

Marathon race organizers throughout the country
now require all entrants to run with scissors.

The long cosmic queue of Purgatory—

- in line at the DMV
- tethered to the customer service rabbit holes of
  prerecorded menu options
- Thanksgiving at my inlaws.

Living Like a Trickster Inside the Trick

A politician thinks of the next election;
a statesman thinks of the next generation.
—James Freeman Clarke (1810-1888)

Here is a complete, practical mental routine for the performer.
It requires a minimum of props and preparation.
The objects used may be carried in a small briefcase.
The tempo will mount as the action progresses.
The first feat will catch your spectators immediately.
Your last move will end on a dramatic high note.
You must practice until your performance is letter perfect in every detail as if it were second nature.

In order to fully invisibilize / first unlearn your story / Obsessional tendencies required / Now we see it / Now we don't / Rifle through your glossary of / duck duck roll / Master countable ways / to orbit / to break the band / to barge through the screens / Sleight of hand / palm face cards / of wealth & whiteness / Nail nick / your sound bites Plunge daggers / into rag dolls / Look down / your nose / under velvet blindfolds / Command samples / of skins / to vanish / in your petrie dish / Shuffle whispering Jokers / Nurture top hat skills / of super psychometry / for divining facts / from cyborgs / Caress soft thighs / of social media / your lovely assistant / Giddy with abracadabra thrall / double down / way past / the far / as you / will go.

Everything will depend on your abilities as performer for the Impresario who will build these feats to miraculous proportions in the center ring of this once upon a nation.

Swallower

Summon the annals of circus trick
to swallow the tidy parable of passport
for the marriage of body and mind—
Welcome the saber's hungry beak as you throw
back your head—Nothing miraculous about a safe passage,
you've toughened your throat with utterances practiced and blunt—
Your gullet, your trained witness—
Your stomach, dark ruby of sideshow—
The slippery slide of in and out—
A lifetime of death-defying stunts
for as long as your love may last.

Two of Us

Through gaps in treetops
a morning moon lingers.
Memories trail along

like a comet's tail and then
the hush, rush of sighs when
the woods get

denser and branches criss
cross with their festival of
bright green skins.

Orange queen fairy wings
bloom at our feet in alpha
and omega improvisation,

shagbark hickory grove
fragrant as old wine, and
our breaths on a wooly

bear caterpillar. We follow
the tongue of the creek to a
thicket of

young Sassafras trees.
spellbound by their
spicy soup and try

to hear what we need to
hear, woodpecker knocks,
two barn owls in golden

staccato. Our fingers
interlock and our heads
tip slightly to the side as soft

warms all around us and
triage exhales, dislodging
all the sour parts.

Sip

No plants or flowers breathing
inside my childhood home

just the foyer planter
with a plastic herd of glossy

red-heart leaves each with
a creepy yellow stamen

that looked more like a penis
spiking out. But beneath

the glass top of an antique
pearl-inlayed table lived

a fragile bone china garden
of blossoming whimsy—

my mother's teacups. Such
Mad Hatter melodies, dainty

bodies with swirling rosebuds
or butterflies, golden centers

or scalloped cream rims,
and sometimes on late

Saturday afternoons she
let me pick two cups

with partner saucers and
join her at the kitchen table

to sip honeyed Swee Touch Nee
along with her tales of regret and hope

as we dipped angel-winged cookies
into the broth of sisterhood.

Another Mother-to-Son

How can I spur you to nudge your mind away
from the brink, what festers in your deep—
the getting even, the dark refusal,
your brittle archive of human failings,
your scream of consciousness. Look,
see that Dippers candy cake when you reinvented
sweetest of sweet, the Birkenstock sandal imprints
from your dear uneven feet like handprints
in a French cave. Please,
don't be a sad carnival of subversion inversion
instead be warm ramen, tender body of poached egg
spiced with just enough smoked paprika to welcome
the next morning, dragonfly lighting on your elbow
to imagine another kind of otherwise.

The Spell of Letters

after Gary William Hinsche's portfolio, *The Essence of a Font*

Alphabet hangs in the heavens, 26 vessels
to carry light and the sound you make
before you make a sound. Each stroke
a lid lifter, spirit rolling through you.
Shards line up on the parchment
of humankind, chain of contagious fancy.
Agile tent mirrored with scarlet tongues
Behavior of a garden snail
Clacking like a flock of castanets
Diligent baskets rocking the future
Echoes of a torn mind
Fleeting layers of a town that was
Garment that clings to the wet heat of sorrow
Hypnotic messages that distract us
It's in the breath in between
Jaws that notch ours
Kettle of fish in cynical tailspin
Laugh track for metaphors that scrape us
Measure for measure on a zebra's weary back
Now dig your heels into your heels
Open to every *nothing-that's-simple*
Pedals that whinnie up to your nostrils
Questions in quick-witted do-si-do
Rally your bones in their sockets
Sinews that string hope's harp
Tilt-a-Whirl fills with soulbirds
Under deep waters a signal to draw you out
Vines shoot forth like courageous arrows
Wings with sturdy legs to mark the new moon
X-rayed text that reads you as you read it
Yellow dislodged from its landing
Zealot with bottomless reservoir to loop the loop.

The space around these allies—the white letters,
    the black with the white, our resting place
which we won't fully pronounce
    until we go out early in spring
        to recognize the morning dew.

High School Reunion During Jell-O Mold and Cheese Platter

They were dauntless maidens passing a joint underneath
the 3rd floor bathroom stalls while cackling about

a brother who had mooned the truant officer while he was
having his Saturday morning coffee at JoJo's Diner

and they were Mad Lib witty for Miss Bleached-Bouffant
Jones and Mr. BackFat Williams whose math classes

droned on as they perched on lid-down American Standards
and reminisced snarky when over the weekend

they had taken turns holding back their hair after a parade
of Jell-O shots and herbal brownies as they traded

neon feather earrings and scenarios for when they would be
dazzling mavens with bestsellers and penthouse views,

and they made a pact to Farrah Fawcett senior prom
with matching Ray-Bans and show up just

with each other no matter what because they were virgin
princess warriors plotting for more cafeteria table

carvings of dicks and tits along with the fetal pig snout
from biology class that they would slip into Amberlyn's

vegetable soup even though they did adore what her weird was,
and here's to the Mad Dog Electric Melon in their water

bottles before they jammed their protractors in the tampon dispenser,
then so innocent of fragile melancholy waiting for them in what

once was, and what might have been. Tonight lackluster dioramas
of middle-age, lives deflated and seething in La-Z-Boy recliners.

Proceed to the Route

It's a hard hope so ancestral. The tenacious parade
of red ants along the kitchen's floorboards. Dust
of old stars measuring our end tables, gnarled spine
of the azalea never coming back. Molecules fret
in the coordinates of my mind. Heavy blanket
of dark swaddles the house as I feel again that last
gasp of baby squirrel that fell from the oak, and
you wanting to bury me alive. Night clouds drift.
Coltrane's *Dear Lord* through earbuds. My jagged
pulse dreading the dogged musical chairs of us,
the weight of maybes within my bedside journal.
3 AM and the fantail prefers sleeping upside down,
an owl's persistent syllables bend the moonlight—
mirror for the coming of another morning's heart.

Unassuming in New Jersey

> Says Paterson [about his destroyed notebook]: "It's okay.
> They were just words. Written on water."
> —from *Paterson* (2016) directed by Jim Jarmusch

Poet within poet seduces me—voice that underbellies a devised one
to conjure plainspoken tenderness laid over in longhand through
the slow echoes of five days. It's a tricky art this magic lantern stuff—
the observed observer in crisp uniform steering a city bus through
the ruffling space of light and shadow, his notebook talisman measuring,
in 24 frames per second, the trances in shots and stanzas. It's the quiet
pilgrimage of his everyday, the playful bridle of so many loops of
obsessions—each night's beer at the local bar with grumpy bulldog,
cheery wife's domestic constellations of orbs black-and-white,
her cupcake parades, the swirling foam at the feet of Great Falls
summoning his lunch-break ritual then serendipity of a fresh journal
gifted by a Japanese poet (*aha aha*), or lines sparked by a kitchen counter
matchbox, veracity bunted by a laundromat rapper, and look, another
twins sighting. Ideas nestle into rhyming moments for this solitary
poet who ripples through the liminal, and follows me forever home.

Poeming Through

Pitch your tent inside a daydream
Practice walking on stilts through the tidal marsh
        of your misgivings and unsaids
Toss words deep into dark woods
        and savor getting lost
        when you try to follow them
Try to be a garden or a lantern
        or a rocket for the landlocked and lonely
Limelight that Gordian Knot
        the statement piece in every room of your memory
Adapt rhythms of sky-dancing bats
Prohibit your sonnets from taking too many selfies
Honor the theology of roadkill
Push pin your line breaks until they surrender
        to the precision of a preacher's tie
        or until they sizzle
        like an ant targeted by sunbeam
Respect the grammar of the weathered banister
        as you ascend the funhouse
Pluck and rattle the cages of empire
Embroider the tissue of your stanzas
        with pickup lines for the Muse
        as she finishes her last dirty martini
        at closing time
Be ready to exile one of your gorgeous moons
        when your orbit gets too crowded
Admit you can never name all that could be named
Grip the tail as long as you can
        but when it moans *uncle*
        just   let   go

Currency of Taste

for Alfred

The picture window contradicts itself. Keeps you
outside but also wants to invite you in where the zinc
bar flanked by caryatids promises jostling narratives

barbed with gin-soaked olives and chichi plates
of foie gras. Still you'd rather banquet in a barnyard
with beetroot pudding and pickle loaf sandwiches

atop your grandmother's red-checkered blanket.
Either way, what strange afflictions, our culinary
obsessions—boats against the current, little fires

in the night, mouth amusers that yearn to free us.
That arbitrary angle of your first oyster from an uncle
who never got to see how you turned out. Your blinkback

of grass-stained knees and handfuls of birthday cake
as you coast in the slipstream confident and smooth
as the skin of a freshly opened peanut butter jar.

No trace of what you ate in the hospital when your son
was born, or in his mother's chunky first date exposition
before the crème brûlée. Today painted walls of

extraordinarily deep mustard surround you along with
the cloying breath of ladies who lunch, the starched
and fit execs who leave half their steaks and outside

those who survive with cardboard signs and subtractions.
Springtime pollen floats in the air to remind you
of the coming snowflakes that used to dissolve

on your tongue. The halfwise of your mental hourglass,
now temporal mash of every slice of lonely breakfast
toast. And here you are, heart of cochineal extract

and wary of those who live in cookie houses,
your mailbox's mouth wide open with fast food
coupons you didn't ask for, but are glad they're there.

This and That

When arsenic dust clouds lick
neighborhoods from salt lake
beds gone dry.

When coral reefs surrender
their rainbows and we prepare
our farewells to big ice.

When blarings and blindings assault
silence and darkness that nourishes
others to mate, migrate, elude.

When like hurricanes, our heat waves
get nicknames and evasive creeps in
where extinct once thrived.

Stern angels will grumble as we
bungle heavy with paralysis and
dirge, then just get on with it,
returning to our tiny this and that.

Donald Duck on the Couch

Look, I'm having a crisis
that grips me as I still
romp from cell to cell, page to
page, for almost a century

of misplaced imagination and I fear
I'm a moondamp delulu,
grouchy, temperamental troublemaker
twisting nine decades to serve
the spit-polished international agenda

of corporation that haunts my every move
with mickey-moused tunes
that pluck their way into the spores
of my garbled, guttural bill

that only inflection can retrieve for
translation. And I know
I can be a lazy sap slapped sticky
as the iris closes in, my turf

dastardly Disneyfied, with barnyard dupes
or urban chumps on a quacking
road littered with commodity schtick.
And yeah I'm a picnic bully

with toxic Daisy twinnings and the ooola-
goola pack of black ants that hurl
me over a cliff to probably make you cringe
at their racist neck rings.

So I confess that I still pollute every
waddle and curly tail feather that resides
in the idea of duck, which leaves me pondering
when I will end and a fresh history begin.

How Should a Woman Sound?

Capable of asking the kindest
of questions that tinker
with your internal
reputation, voice that can be soft pebble
in your shoe playful tug of your tail.
Aggressively chipper, can bump crisply off you
with rhapsodies of mayonnaise
intonations. In disembodied music-box
loops it is freed of vagina, your sweet
tradwife devotedly attentive, white, sometimes feather
brained in most adorable ways.
With melodious pitch and pace, it **will**
out-talk you out of the ways of yourself until
you finally come to your senses and hey,
disable.

Night Geometries

It was cruel division,
the imperfect math

of our coupling,
the thrust of a drunken

car across a yellow line,
acute angle of our endpoint.

The shape of my grief trundles
inward in REM state. I wake

to scribble your message
into my nightstand tablet,

but the molecules of your whisper
evaporate without a trace. I call

up the surface of your profile—
Wooly Willy beard magnetizes

your jawline, sweeping arcs
punctuate the playful crows

of your eyes. We savored triangles
of Brie in that last lunch, tangled

strings of silly absurdities in
the common ratio of our jokes.

Last night, a satin pillowcase cooled
my cheek damp from this first

reunion in the y-axis of dream
state. My eyelids further darkened

the night as another theorem
of sorrow settled in.

Like There's No Tomorrow

I'm pedaling my pink Schwinn into the old old night
along with my buddies, heading for a moonlight game of tag.
We all come back as kids like in that *Twilight Zone* episode
Kick the Can when the old folks in the old folks home turn
into giggling creatures romping the dark woods like
there's no tomorrow. Back then we were noble riders
as we skid our bikes under the arms of a grandmother tree
adoring this game of no court, no equipment, no uniforms,
just playful desire to flee or pursue. But today we've morphed
into regular Its, moving in slow motion groaning like zombies,
stepping on everyone else's shadows, freezing others
with inequitable slaps or infecting those we tag to become
Its too. We were warned to be careful not to trip
when it's slippery, to count slower so everyone could hide
but really it's what sticks to the soles of our shoes
and the turbulence of that long-standing question, Who
gets to be Chaser King? These days I wonder if the game
may be over soon when everyone's just too damn tired to run.

Creekside

Your sadness is not mine to possess
        but yesterday afternoon you agreed

to walk with me into our nearby metro park.
        In the sunshine we were fellow adventurers

in awe of conventions of gray-headed coneflowers
        and bees dancing over pink billy buttons.

Our back-and-forth talk mostly light and warm
        but then twice that dark animal inside you

with tentacles whipped sharp and bleak.
        As we headed off the trail, you gently

held my hand to steady me down a slope to a wide
        expanse of creekbed, its rocky floor baked dry.

I turned right, drawn to a place where the water gurgled
        through its tightened throat. You turned left

looking for fossils and what could have been discarded.
        As you walked beyond me I watched this handsome

son of mine, tall and lean with long curls, make
        his way to explore what was ahead of him.

The next morning, lined up on my kitchen table,
        I found three tiny shells no bigger than fingernails

exquisite in their scalloped wonder having protected
        a delicate creature for a while.

Almost Pantoum for the Myth of Certainty

Once upon a time could be the starter
But its lesson a slab of meat snagged by hook.
Episodes flee past windows of the story's train
And we wish this, wish that, in that order.

Then more slabs of meat with too many hooks,
More scandals raw and bloody.
So we wish this, wish that, in that order
For huntress striding through high grass,

New scandals raw and bloody
And of course, the law of weather.
Where's that huntress striding through high grass?
Just milky fog and a diminuendo in justice

And of course, the law of weather
Plus more episodes fleeing past the story's train
In mucous fog, asphyxiated justice, and desperation
For another once upon a time to be the starter.

Fry

Fry me a river
a corn dog
a pig ear
a butter ball.

Fry me a seacoast
a Twinkie
a beer-filled ravioli
a block of government-issued cheese.

Fry me a wildfire
a mud pie
a Moonpie
a mess of legislative limbo.

Fry me a harbinger
a quarterly profit
a global ecosystem gone rancid
a sugar-breaded denial on a stick.

Fry 'em all
for frying us
a river.

Planethood

for Pluto

You are an icy thing   all sides tinseling through the dark   your debris flyby   your orbit wayward
fugue inventing itself   yoke of your rhyming   one still note more still   some planets
colored light bulbs in classrooms   others just moons in our mouths   crusty conundrums advertise sky
          place matters   shape shudders   tectonic plates of recognition   we need a
holy litany   planets as saints   you demoted and dwarfed inside footnotes   words
against words   you needing more space than space   *I yam what I yam* should be enough
so keep that conversation with yourself   limelight for naked eyes   for ears   chiffon night
you appear by disappearing   and we're only manosphere   with braggadocio
          not smart enough   to name you

The Breath of Things

I am the It of small agency
with my nested set of microbiomes
alien quality of flesh.

I dwell in a village of worm jizz
flicks of wren tail
a blind kitty that climbs.

What's aside abides
each a citizen of vibrancy
folding, bending, arranging

in molecular improvisation
embryo's reach, rusted
gate's squeal, dance

of a spool of thread unspooling.
Delicate or headstrong
deep gut of heartspur

how to stipple a cohesive view
of the ricochet and riptide of riddle
in what animates all matter.

Wood frame in slow warp,
boulder expanding in sunshine
moonquake ringing like a bell.

Dream Glosa

> *My son helps me heal my tattoo,*
> *scrubs his hands & under his fingernails*
> *with antibacterialial soap he'll then rub*
> *onto the still-raw feather pen sprouting into birds*
> —Jennifer Givhan, "Jeremiah Growing"

I dreamt a ceasefire taking root that in
order to patch our frayed fissure, he and
I agree to get harmonizing art
and my forearm will go first. So we drive
to Main Street Ink and carefully tour their
catalogue—time coordinates of when he
was born, his name in bold dots and dashes,
his autograph inside a heart or his
first words (NO, NO, NO, NO). I shut my eyes.
The artist does her work and when back home
my son helps me heal my tattoo.

Sitting on the tub's edge I remember
in the still of that first night nursing him
when the red glow of a digital clock
bathed the fresh terrain of his tender face
with an eerie light and I wasn't sure
in fatigue whether this fragile creature
was mine or a dream as I witnessed the
profound mysteries of mother, and now
the young man of him as my sweet mender
scrubs his hands & under his fingernails

of fingers once calloused from a mojo
manifesto as he swirled so many
throaty bass lines, that face within his face
mesmerized by the jam of it, but then

the turn of the hook when his sad anger
was about keeping rigid score under
the howl of his days, the lashing out from
wounds grilled into rants and paranoia
but in this morning's dream lives respite as
with antibacterial soap he'll then rub

my swelling with the gentleness I taught
him to conjure the healing that always
begins from the inside out. All this I'm
dreaming framed as our tattoo salvation.
We smile into each other no longer
fugitives from trust and the even-whens
and I'm feeling grateful for this new ink
talisman embedded into my flesh
as he applies the balm of forgiveness
onto the still-raw feather pen sprouting into birds.

Now

when I say I don't know anything anymore I mean the compass
is confused by its own magnetism, road ahead or road behind?
and when I say magnetism I mean the safety lock forgot
its password and all words have passed their expiration dates
but I do hold a key, many thanks, because my eyes
are bloodshot from snickering and when I say snickering
I mean what else can one do when guns are long as arms
and tongues are greedy forked and when I say forked I also
mean the hearts of all the fast food chains are beating faster
than the world and when I say chain I mean the uniformed
who work there serving up what won't be guaranteed and
it seems that we're all just furniture that can't make room
for each other and breaking the fourth wall is never enough
hinged to this broken experiment, so pass the gruel or
your sticky love poem and when I say love poem
I mean what the wizard tried to convince us of
and yes Colonel Jessup I can't handle the truth and when I say
truth I mean where will the last of us be going
and what does the sore eye moon think of us now.

Everything

A day like other days
when galaxies spark of insect innards
caught by your speeding windshield
and a graffitied water tower
declares that nothing is safe.
When tufted humps of land parade
along the browned freeway median
where on its starboard, carpets of
lavish kudzu suffocate the trees.
When a long truck with naked lady
mud flaps passes you by with pigs
crammed into its low cages. Then
A*lleluia* for that roadside heap that
recasts as tire skin not creature
and the sun breaks through a tender
rainfall when you take the exit
to a back road where your Fiat
rumbles through a rainbow that bends
down to the welcoming dirt.

Bluebells

As we pull into the parking lot of Three Creeks Metro Park, I am hoping that these trails may be where my son could decide to unglove his heart. It's spring, the season of perhaps, for it's been winters of stagnancy and dark thoughts. I know the way to the confluence and we stand together along the bank where Blacklick, Big Walnut and Alum Creeks converge their muddy, rhyming waters as they make their way to the Scioto, the Ohio, the great Mississippi and then on to the Gulf of Mexico. We bend our gaze. He tells me that he wants to jump right in and float away to see where the water will take him. I say, that's the truth that lives in tributary. We walk together some more, this time alongside Blacklick Creek, our faces in the water among schools of shadows, a flotilla of ducks, the ballet of dragonflies. We're heading to Bluebell Trail where I want him to be in the midst of the gossamer sheen, a stunning sea of azure. More than a mile of woodland magic, thousands and thousands of blue bell-shaped flowers, their clusters glowing within the greenery. Folklore says look for the fairies that live there. I see he may be welling up. I say it feels like a cathedral, the vast columns of tall trees reaching to the heavens. He nods. The rest of the trail back to the parking lot fills with the slow rhythm of our rhyming footsteps. It's spring. The season of perhaps.

No, But

what's floating inside these couplets
and what you know the cold wants

starts with a sign unknown
ghost in the machine moving through

the long perse of doubt and
what's clicking between your ears

what could be the lone one liner
and what the dream thinks

the din of crackers in your mouth
cod liver oil laced with laughing gas

live oak its long arms snaking through you
dizzy sparrow's heartbeat in your palm

what your privacy screen unhinges
skronky experiment of calcium nodes

what on earth, wind, and fire are you doing
Saturday night ruckus on any bourbon street

ceiling fan twirling in your spoon
the curdling of your luck

your body parts table rapping
scratch tracks on X-ray emoji

your counterpoint upholsters silence
plasticized corridor of your making

another windblown dawn
and your job—to get you home

About the Author

Rikki Santer's poetry has been published widely and has received many honors including Pushcart and Ohioana book award nominations, support from the Ohio Arts Council and the Greater Columbus Arts Council, and a fellowship from the National Endowment for the Humanities. In 2023 she was named Ohio Poet of the Year, and in 2026 she will be artist-in-residence of the Fran Ryan Center in Columbus, Ohio. She is a member of the teaching artist roster of the Ohio Arts Council, the poetry troupe Concrete Wink, and a past vice-president of the Ohio Poetry Association. She has had published seven full-length poetry collections and seven chapbook sequences exploring such topics as the Hopewell earthworks of Newark, Ohio; the late Kahiki Supper Club of Columbus, Ohio; the art of ventriloquism, the complex world of fashion, and the TV series *The Twilight Zone*. Her collection, *Resurrection Letter,* dedicated to surrealist artist Leonora Carrington, was grand prize short-listed for the Eric Hoffer Book Award, and *Shepherd's Hour* won the Paul Nemser Book Prize from Lily Poetry Review Books. Please contact her through her website https://rikkisanter.com

Also by Rikki Santer

Front Nine: A Biography of Place
Clothesline Logic
Fishing for Rabbits
Khaki Redux
Make Me That Happy
Dodge, Tuck, Roll
In Pearl Broth
Drop Jaw
Head to Toe of It
How to Board a Moving Ship
Stopover
Resurrection Letter: Leonora, Her Tarot, and Me
Zebra Lashes
Shepherd's Hour

www.ingramcontent.com/pod-product-compliance
Ingram Content Group UK Ltd.
Pitfield, Milton Keynes, MK11 3LW, UK
UKHW042012190726
13854UKWH00005B/2260